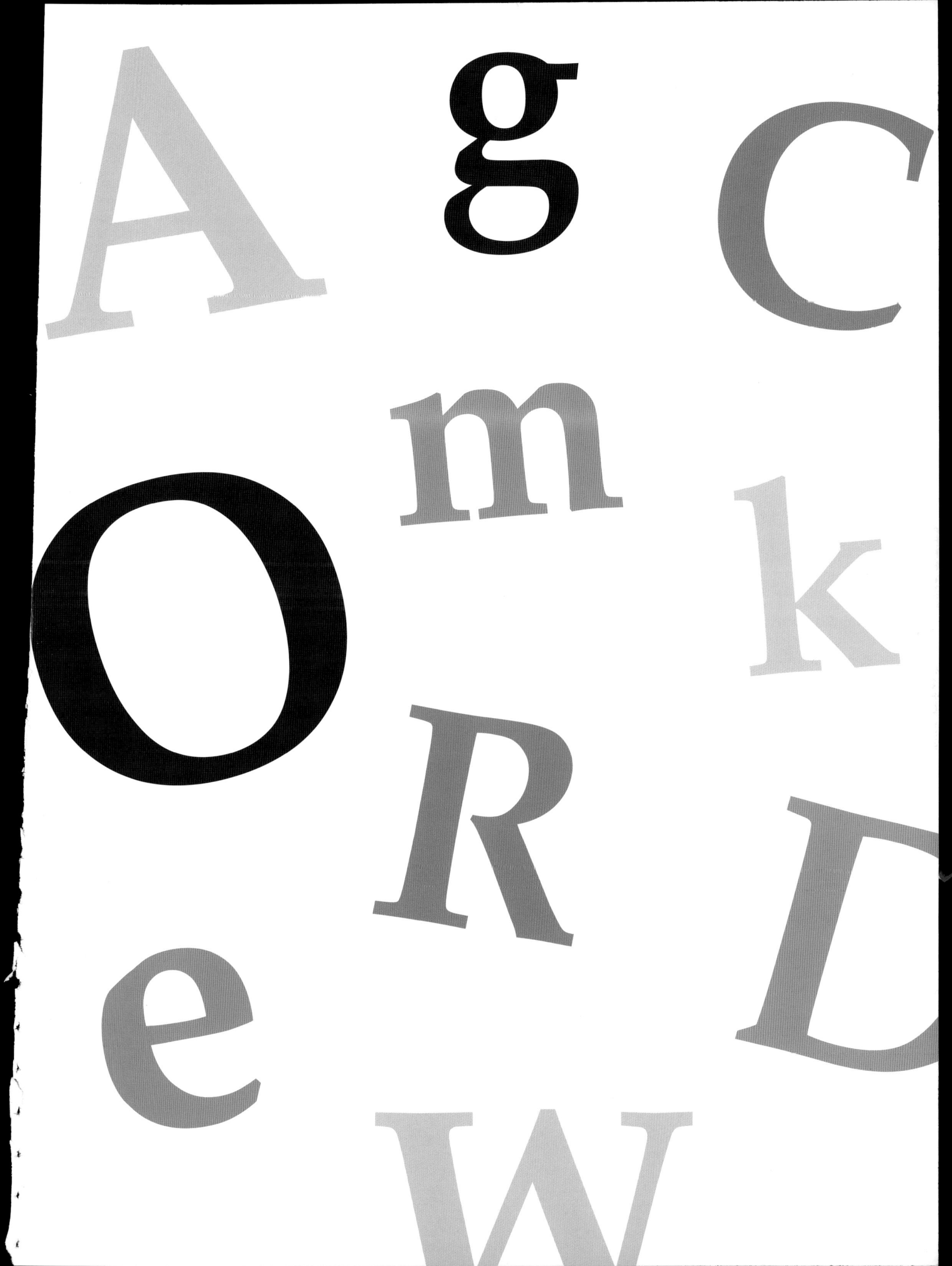

Published by Creative Education
123 South Broad Street, Mankato, Minnesota 56001

Creative Education is an imprint of The Creative Company.
Design by Stephanie Blumenthal
Production design by The Design Lab
Art direction by Rita Marshall

Photographs by Corbis (Academy of Natural Sciences of Philadelphia, B.S.P.I., Blue Lantern Studio, Horace Bristol, Macduff Everton, John Henley, Francis G. Mayer, John McAnulty, Christopher J. Morris, Carl & Ann Purcell, Kevin Schafer, Leonard de Selva), Getty Images (Gary Buss)

Library of Congress Cataloging-in-Publication Data

Fandel, Jennifer.
Metaphors, similes, and other word pictures / by Jennifer Fandel.
p. cm. — (Understanding poetry)
ISBN 978-1-58341-340-1
1. Metaphor—Juvenile literature. 2. Simile—Juvenile literature. 3. Poetics—Juvenile literature. I. Title. II. Understanding poetry (Mankato, Minn.)

PN1059.M4F36 2004
808.1—dc22 2004058223

4 6 8 9 7 5 3

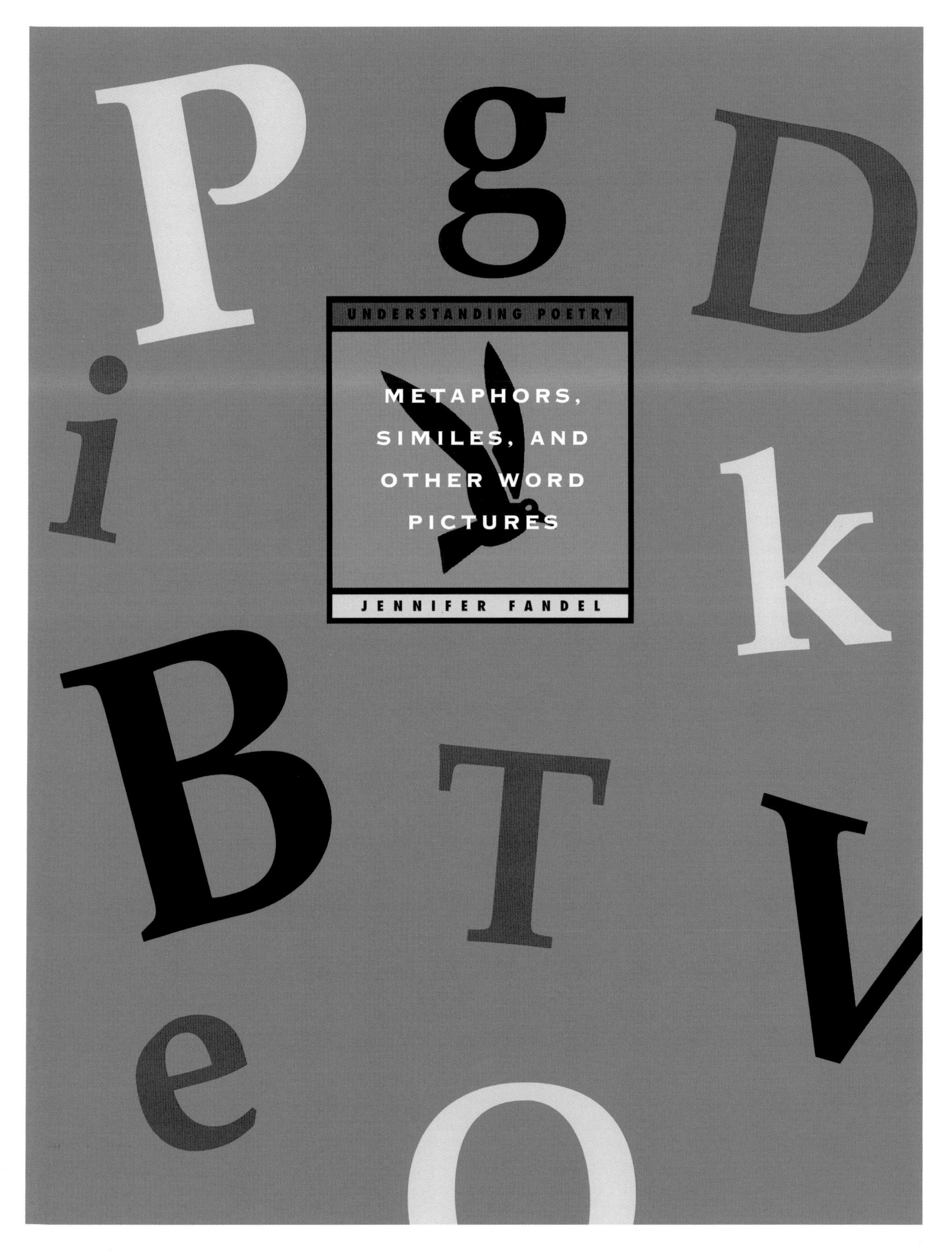

CREATIVE EDUCATION

It's a beautiful day. The sky is the brightest shade of blue, the trees sway in the breeze, and patches of clouds float overhead. When some people see a sight like this, they might take a photograph or paint a picture to help them remember it. Others might lie on their back with a friend and talk about the shapes of the clouds. And there are others who might write a poem about it. All people have a desire to share their visions, feelings, and ideas. But what makes people write poetry? People who express themselves through poetry often love the images, meanings, and sounds of words.

Just like painting, music, sculpture, and dance, poetry is a powerful art form that can touch people's minds and hearts. Poems can tell a story, teach people, express emotions, celebrate language, and much more. When you listen to or read a poem, you'll likely discover something new about the world or yourself. And when you write poetry, you'll probably learn more about the way you see and understand the world around you. It's the joy of discovery that makes people return to a blank notebook page day after day, hoping to fill it with poetry.

Before societies had written languages, people often communicated through pictures, called pictograms, drawn on cave walls. People told stories and shared poems, but they had to rely on their memories to do so. In many ways, they used their minds just like they used the cave walls. Pictures stayed etched in their memories, helping them to recall the words of a story or poem. It was probably from that time, in the earliest societies, that word pictures came to be.

Word pictures are one of the most important tools poets use to create poems. Through the use of images, poets can show their experiences. More importantly, word pictures invite readers to step inside the poem and inside the poet's mind. When you use word pictures, you have the power to bring others into your life and into your imagination, showing them the world through your eyes.

The Image in Imagination

When you use your imagination, you think in terms of **concrete** things you've seen or experienced. For example, you might remember a time when you felt sad. Your imagination, though, doesn't think the word "sad" over and over again. Instead, you recall images that make you remember that sadness. It could be a broken umbrella on a rainy day, a meal of all your least favorite foods, or a crumpled note that ended a friendship. And these word pictures, or images, make your sadness come alive, helping you feel the emotions again. And just as these images affect you, they will also affect your audience (the people who hear or read your poetry). Your audience might not have experienced the same exact sadness that you write about, but your images will help them better understand your feelings.

The first step in writing images is to think about things that you can see. By writing down the **details** of a certain moment, you can help recreate it for your readers. To get an idea of how this works, let's take a look at a very short poem by William Carlos Williams (1883–1963), an American poet who believed in the importance of images.

THE RED WHEELBARROW

so much depends
upon

a red wheel
barrow

glazed with rain
water

beside the white
chickens.

In "The Red Wheelbarrow," Williams presents a scene to his readers consisting of three things: a wheelbarrow, rainwater, and chickens. Notice how he uses colors (red and white) and descriptive words (glazed and beside) to help readers better imagine the scene. Williams held a belief that the only way to present ideas was through concrete images. Many people debate what this poem is about, but perhaps Williams is simply making the point that there is beauty in simplicity or that images give us insight to the world.

Another poem that uses sight images to create a scene for readers is "The Fish," by an American poet named Elizabeth Bishop (1911–79). In this long poem (part of which appears opposite), Bishop tells a story about how she felt when she caught a fish. Pay special attention to her **descriptions** of the fish and try to imagine the scene she is describing.

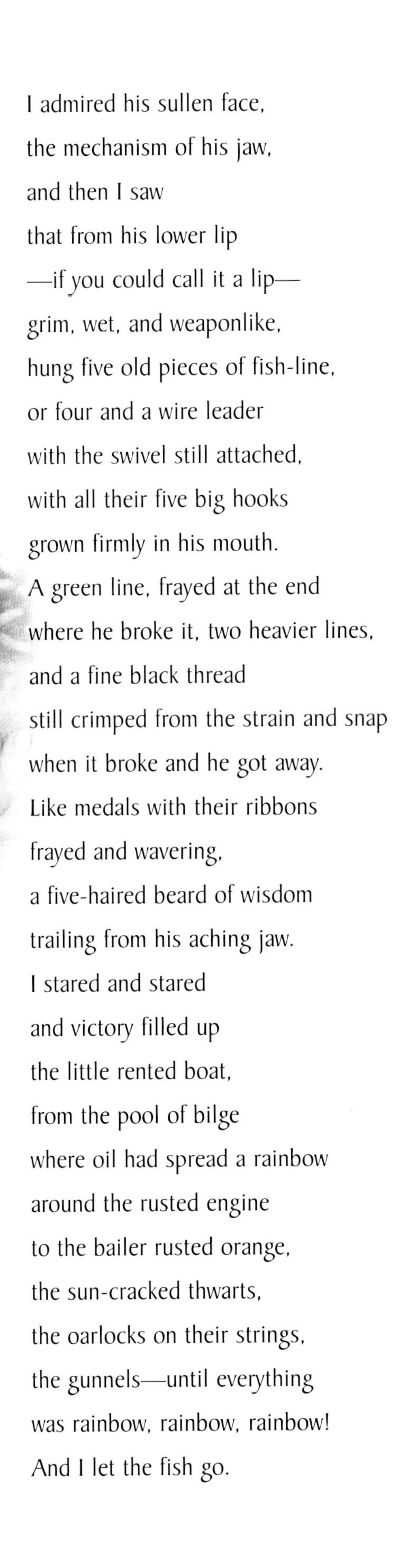

I admired his sullen face,
the mechanism of his jaw,
and then I saw
that from his lower lip
—if you could call it a lip—
grim, wet, and weaponlike,
hung five old pieces of fish-line,
or four and a wire leader
with the swivel still attached,
with all their five big hooks
grown firmly in his mouth.
A green line, frayed at the end
where he broke it, two heavier lines,
and a fine black thread
still crimped from the strain and snap
when it broke and he got away.
Like medals with their ribbons
frayed and wavering,
a five-haired beard of wisdom
trailing from his aching jaw.
I stared and stared
and victory filled up
the little rented boat,
from the pool of bilge
where oil had spread a rainbow
around the rusted engine
to the bailer rusted orange,
the sun-cracked thwarts,
the oarlocks on their strings,
the gunnels—until everything
was rainbow, rainbow, rainbow!
And I let the fish go.

By imagining the world that the poet describes, you can feel what it must have been like to catch such an old, tough fish that had escaped so many catches before. Yet, Bishop also makes us feel like we know this fish. She describes it so well that we don't see it as just any fish. We see it as a specific fish. And through this fish we see the poet's dilemma: Do you keep him, or do you let him go so he can continue his escape-artist life until he eventually dies? Bishop even expresses her decision using an image of rainbows, something that we often think of as meaning peace, new beginnings, and opportunity.

Sight images, such as those in Williams's and Bishop's poems, put readers in the middle of a moment or scene. When you write using sight images, first close your eyes and imagine things as accurately as possible. Think about colors, movements, textures, and where things are located. This description is all part of the world you want your readers to see and imagine. Show readers the strange, brilliant, or ordinary world that you see, and these images will live on in your readers' memories.

World of the Senses

When people think of word pictures, they usually think of things that they can **see**. However, you can also make images using your other four senses: **hearing**, **smell**, **taste**, and **touch**. We call the images that relate to the five senses **sensory** images.

You experience the world through your senses. As a baby, you probably put your rattle in your mouth to learn more about it. You touched someone's beard and smelled your first flower. You listened to music and the laughter of adults. You watched their faces for a smile or searched your toy box for that one bright toy that made you happy. We don't often question how we learned about the world, but the answer lies in the five senses.

To better understand the importance of senses other than sight, take a look at the following poem by American poet William Stafford (1914–93). In his poem, Stafford describes the rich world of sound.

WALKING WITH YOUR EYES SHUT

Your ears receive a platter of sound
heaped where you are, in the center, verging
off at far edges that move as you pass,
like a great hoopskirt of listening through the world.
A brick wall compresses your right ear's horizon
on that side, but the whole sound sky balloons
again all around. A cardinal's whistle
soars up and arcs down behind you. A bluejay
unrolls its part of the day, a long streamer over you,
and then little discs receding smaller and
smaller into the infinity that lives
in the middle of the woods beyond. You carry
this dome all the time. Today you know it,
a great rich room, a musical sky.

It's often said that when people lose one of their senses, the other senses compensate and become even stronger. This definitely seems true in Stafford's poem. By closing his eyes and paying close attention to sound, Stafford notices things that people might normally overlook. He reminds us of this fact when he says, "You carry / this dome all of the time." Additionally, he uses fascinating images, such as "a platter of sound" and "a hoopskirt of listening," to help us imagine what walking with your eyes shut is really like. It's interesting to note that Stafford uses sight images, such as "platter" and "hoopskirt," to describe sound. He also chooses clear direction words ("in the center," "behind you") and strong verbs ("verging," "soars") in his poem. How do these words help you experience the world of sound better? What else does Stafford do to help you imagine the sounds in his poem?

To make people truly experience something, you need to involve their senses. Since you experience the world using all of your senses, you should use as many senses as you can to give readers the same complete experience you had. You feel warm pond water and a baby's soft skin. You taste the spicy heat of your favorite Mexican dinner and your own salty tears. You smell newly cut grass and the sweet freshness of an approaching storm. You hear birds twittering in the morning and car horns blaring during a traffic jam. Anytime you use your imagination, you'll likely start hearing, smelling, tasting, and feeling things, too.

Try walking around with your eyes wide open, with all of your senses at the ready, paying close attention to the little things you normally overlook. It's similar to taking a trip somewhere and experiencing someone else's everyday world for the brilliant place it is. People often take their own neighborhood for granted. They stop noticing all of its unique strangeness and beauty. If you pretend that you're on a trip as you walk through your day, chances are you will notice amazing things that have been right in front of you all along. This is the stuff that poems are made of!

What Similes Are Like

Poets write with the hope that readers will understand and relate to their feelings and ideas. But this is sometimes hard, since people have different experiences, cultures, and backgrounds. You probably haven't fought in a war, but that shouldn't stop you from understanding what a war might be *like*. You probably don't have a full-time job or a family to feed, but you might understand what that experience is *like*. A special type of image, called a **simile**, tells readers what things "are like" so that they can better relate to the experience in the poem.

The word "simile" comes from the Latin word for "like." When you write a simile, you use the words like or as to make a comparison between two things.

You might tell readers, for example, that "love is like a big wet dog that shakes water all over you. You know what's coming but you can't get away from it." This simile helps readers get a better idea of how you see love, especially since love is something that is different for every person. You might also describe someone's hair as being "as dry and fuzzy as moss." By comparing the hair to moss, readers can better picture just how dry and fuzzy it is. Or you might help readers understand what it was like to lose someone you loved by providing images that take you back to that feeling. Close your eyes and let images come back to you. What did things look *like*? What did they sound *like*? What did they smell *like*, taste *like*, or feel *like*?

To better understand similes, let's look at the poem "Harlem," by African-American poet Langston Hughes (1902–67). In the poem, Hughes uses powerful similes to help readers understand the feelings of blacks struggling and dreaming of equal rights when blacks didn't have the right to vote and weren't treated the same as whites. (The word "deferred" in the poem means "put off until later.")

HARLEM

What happens to a dream deferred?

Does it dry up
like a raisin in the sun?
Or fester like a sore—
And then run?
Does it stink like rotten meat?
Or crust and sugar over—
like a syrupy sweet?

Maybe it just sags
like a heavy load.

Or does it explode?

Hughes uses five strong similes in this short poem. Do they seem positive or negative to you? How do you think Hughes felt about having his dream deferred? Even if you didn't live through the civil rights struggle of the early to mid-1900s, you can probably understand how many African-Americans felt. It's the power of Hughes's similes that helps us feel what this experience was like.

There is a problem that often comes up when people begin writing poetry: **clichés** (klee-SHAYZ). While the word sounds harmless enough, it's something to avoid in your writing. Clichés are overused images that people have heard over and over again, such as "slow as a turtle" or "bright as the sun." You may think to yourself, "If I use these similes, people will know exactly what I'm talking about." That may be partly true, but you risk losing your audience's interest because you aren't telling them anything new. Readers want to be surprised by fresh images. They want to see the world in a new way.

The famous English poet and playwright William Shakespeare (1564–1616) certainly surprised readers with the following **sonnet**. Tired of love poems that compared women to sunshine, roses, and goddesses, Shakespeare decided to play with these clichés and tell readers how he really saw the woman he loved. (Below, the word "dun" means "brown," "damasked" means "of mixed colors," and "reeks" means "exhales.")

SONNET 130

My mistress' eyes are nothing like the sun;
Coral is far more red than her lips' red;
If snow be white, why then her breasts are dun;
If hairs be wires, black wires grow on her head.
I have seen roses damasked, red and white,
But no such roses see I in her cheeks;
And in some perfumes is there more delight
Than in the breath that from my mistress reeks.
I love to hear her speak, yet well I know
That music hath a far more pleasing sound;
I grant I never saw a goddess go;
My mistress, when she walks, treads on the ground.
And yet, by heaven, I think my love as rare
As any she belied with false compare.

Shakespeare's sonnet is memorable because he pokes fun at clichés. Shakespeare doesn't see his love's eyes "as bright as the sunshine" or her cheeks "as red as roses." Instead, he tells us that the woman he loves is unique and unlike anything that has been described before. Remember, one of the most important parts of writing poetry is keeping your readers interested by surprising them. Don't ignore the images around you. There are great similes just waiting to be written!

METAPHOR: WHAT THINGS *ARE*

Another important type of image is the **metaphor**. The word "metaphor" comes from the Greek word for transfer. It's similar to the simile, but it doesn't use "like" or "as" to make a comparison. Instead, a metaphor tells readers that "something is something." In other words, a metaphor transfers qualities from one thing to another.

Let's say you wrote the simile "Her skin was as white as the underbelly of a fish." To make this simile into a metaphor, you'd write, "Her skin was the underbelly of a fish." Notice that metaphors have a much different effect than similes do. Metaphors are more direct and perhaps require a little more imagination on the reader's part. Many poets believe that metaphors are stronger images than similes because similes tell readers that two things are similar. Metaphors force readers to see objects joined together, no matter how different they may be.

We can see how metaphors work in a poem by American poet Emily Dickinson (1830–86). In Dickinson's poem, she tells us that hope is a bird, a "thing with feathers." By making this direct comparison, Dickinson helps readers see hope in the same way we see a tireless sparrow. The bird faces many hardships—weathering storms and rebuilding its nest whenever it is destroyed—and yet keeps singing.

254

"Hope" is the thing with feathers—
That perches in the soul—
And sings the tune without the words—
And never stops—at all—

And sweetest—in the Gale—is heard—
And sore must be the storm—
That could abash the little Bird
That kept so many warm—

I've heard it in the chillest land—
And on the strangest Sea—
Yet, never, in Extremity,
It asked a crumb—of Me.

Dickinson's poem would read much differently if she wrote that "hope is like a thing with feathers." Her use of metaphor makes this poem more powerful because readers see the idea of hope entwined with the image of a bird. A simile would only suggest that hope and a bird are related. Dickinson's metaphor, though, tells us that they are the same and inseparable.

Another type of metaphor is made by **personifying** things. People often try to understand the animals, plants, and other objects around them by transferring the characteristics of humans to these objects. A good example of this is seen in the poem "Mushrooms," by American poet Sylvia Plath (1932–63).

MUSHROOMS

Overnight, very
Whitely, discreetly,
Very quietly

Our toes, our noses
Take hold on the loam,
Acquire the air.

Nobody sees us,
Stops us, betrays us;
The small grains make room.

Soft fists insist on
Heaving the needles,
The leafy bedding,

Even the paving.
Our hammers, our rams,
Earless and eyeless,

Perfectly voiceless,
Widen the crannies,
Shoulder through holes. We

Diet on water,
On crumbs of shadow,
Bland-mannered, asking

Little or nothing.
So many of us!
So many of us!

We are shelves, we are
Tables, we are meek,
We are edible,

Nudgers and shovers
In spite of ourselves.
Our kind multiplies:

We shall by morning
Inherit the earth.
Our foot's in the door.

Do mushrooms have noses or toes? Do they know that people often overlook them since they grow in hidden places? Do they build relationships with each other or plan their future? We know that the answer to these questions is no, but the personification of the mushrooms helps us see them in a new way. We imagine that they feel things—such as loneliness or neglect—as we feel them. And we imagine that they have human body parts. Personification is an important type of imagery that can help readers understand the world around them.

Clichés can pose a problem when a poet works with metaphors, but **mixed metaphors**

are often the bigger problem. Mixed metaphors happen when images give readers conflicting views of a subject. For example, you'd probably be confused if a person were called both a wild dog and a graceful cat in the same poem. Or you might stop and think a while if you read that the stars in the sky were bright fire and cold ice. In these examples, the different images work against each other and may confuse your readers. In the following short poem, "Fog," American poet Carl Sandburg (1878–1967) compares the movement of fog to the movement of a cat.

Sandburg's poem does not contain a mixed metaphor, but imagine that Sandburg had said that the fog "comes on big elephant feet." When we read the second stanza of the poem, we'd be confused, because we had already pictured the fog as heavy and noisy. These conflicting images would not work well together.

Anytime you use metaphors, you want your ideas to fit together smoothly to give your reader a clear view of your subject. Experiment with this powerful type of image, and your readers will almost certainly enjoy it!

FOG

The fog comes
on little cat feet.

It sits looking
over harbor and city
on silent haunches
and then moves on.

Abstract Ideas, Concrete Images

Poets often express ideas and emotions in poems through images. Images allow poets to talk about **abstract** things in a way that is concrete, or touchable. These concrete images open our eyes to larger meanings by helping us focus on specific things that we understand.

Most people have heard the old phrase "Beauty is in the eye of the beholder." What this phrase means is that everyone's idea of beauty is different. Because of this, you need to describe people, places, and objects to help readers understand your version of beauty. Readers would have a hard time imagining beauty if they were simply told "Wanda is beautiful" or "The mountains are beautiful." That's because "beautiful" is an abstract word. Abstract words tell readers of a quality (such as beauty) or condition (such as sadness), but they don't help readers see it. That's what concrete images are for. You might tell readers that Wanda has eyes that scrunch up when she laughs, or you might tell them that the mountains were covered in clouds that split apart to reveal the sunshine. These concrete images would help readers see your vision of beauty.

Contemporary American poet Adrienne Rich (1931–) helps readers understand the abstract idea of "loneliness" in her poem "Song." You might easily relate to some of the concrete images that Rich uses to describe loneliness.

SONG

You're wondering if I'm lonely:
OK then, yes, I'm lonely
as a plane rides lonely and level
on its radio beam, aiming
across the Rockies
for the blue-strung aisles
of an airfield on the ocean

You want to ask, am I lonely?
Well, of course, lonely
as a woman driving across country
day after day, leaving behind
mile after mile
little towns she might have stopped
and lived and died in, lonely

If I'm lonely
it must be the loneliness
of waking first, of breathing
dawn's first cold breath on the city
of being the one awake
in a house wrapped in sleep

If I'm lonely
it's with the rowboat ice-fast on the shore
in the last red light of the year
that knows what it is, that knows it's neither
ice nor mud nor winter light
but wood, with a gift for burning

When Rich describes loneliness, does it sound like something terrible? Or do you think that loneliness is something that Rich simply accepts about life? Pay close attention to the concrete images she uses. Do you feel lonely when you are the first person awake in the house, or do you like this feeling of quiet and peace? Why do you think Rich ended her poem with the image of wood burning? How does that image make you feel?

We all react differently to poems and reach different understandings of them based on our backgrounds and beliefs. For some people, Rich's version of loneliness probably sounds horrible. But to others, the poet's description of loneliness might sound peaceful. In any case, Rich's concrete images help us imagine specific feelings of loneliness. And imagining always helps us understand things better.

Your **mindset** at the time you read a poem can affect your understanding and appreciation of it, and your mindset can also affect you as you write a poem. On a day when you feel happy, for example, you might describe your bedroom as a palace. However, on a day when you feel sad or angry, you might describe your room as a prison cell in which your parents keep you securely locked. Your room stays the same, but how you feel can change how you see it.

Your **emotions** are closely connected to the images in your poems. Just as you should be awake to your senses as you write, you should also be in touch with your emotions. Readers want to understand and feel the way you feel, so let your emotions come through in your imagery.

Show, Don't Tell

For a long time, poets have been giving beginning writers the advice Show, don't tell. Perhaps you've already heard this and have wondered what it really means. These three important words remind writers that they shouldn't simply talk about their experiences on paper. Instead, they should show readers what they experienced. So, for example, instead of telling readers that you fell in love on Tuesday, you should describe what falling in love on Tuesday was like. You want readers to understand your exact feeling by using images, such as similes and metaphors. To help readers understand how you fell in love, you should think about what readers would probably want to imagine. Maybe you could describe how she laughs, tilting her head back. Or you might describe how he walks with a swagger and smiles.

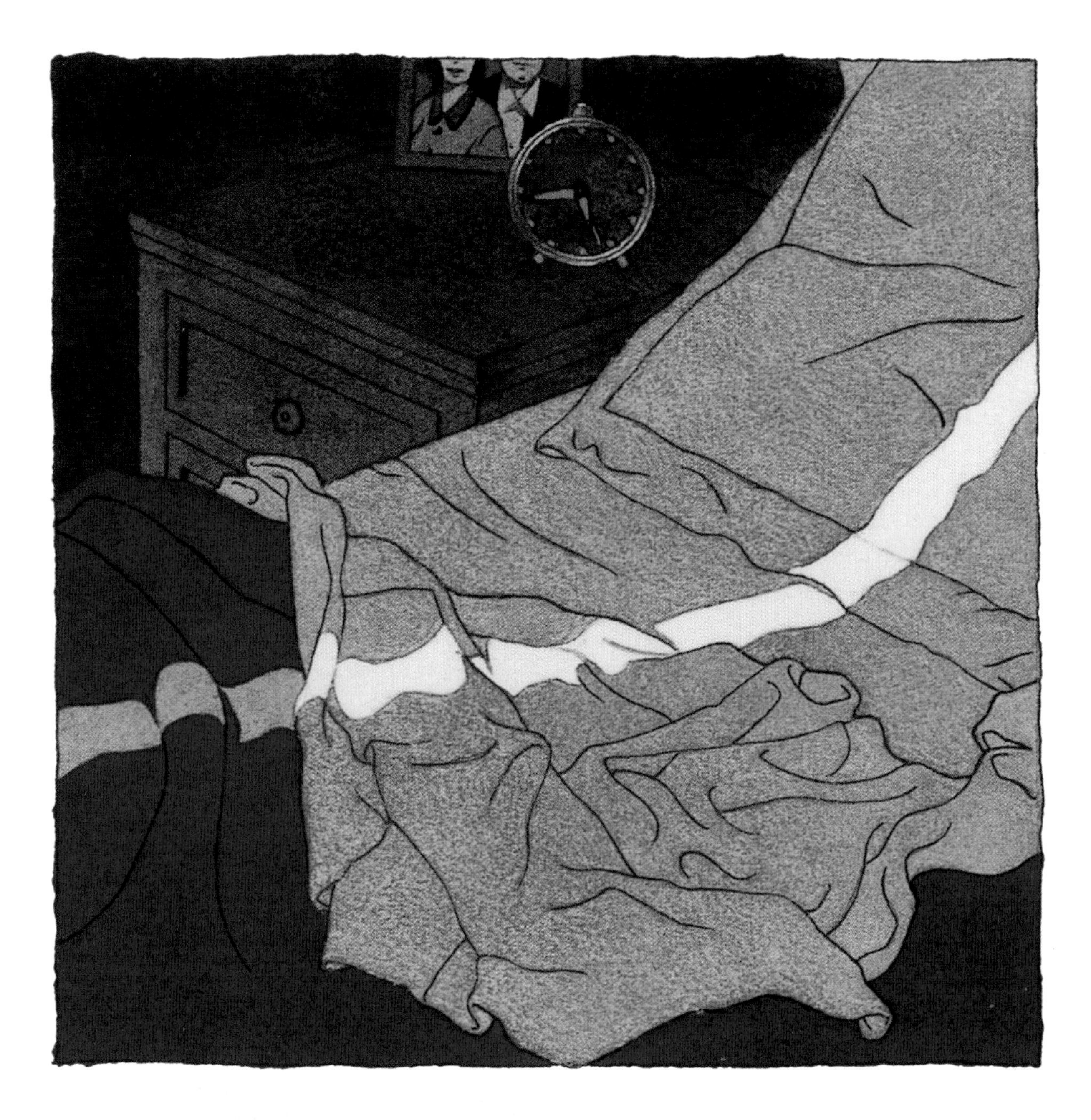

When poets talk about showing, rather than telling, they are also referring to the importance of description over **details**. We often use the words "description" and "detail" as if they mean the same thing, but they are really quite different. Description tries to represent a person, place, or object with information that involves the senses. Details, on the other hand, are very particular bits of information. While some details might be necessary in a poem, they don't help readers visualize the subject you're writing about.

To better understand this difference, imagine you're writing a poem about waking up in the middle of the night. If you use the detail "3 a.m.," readers know the exact time of night. But readers won't be able to imagine that specific night without description. For example, if you described how the clock ticked loudly in the hall, readers would understand how quiet the house was during the night. That would bring the poem to life better than the specific time on the clock. When writing poems, you'll probably select a few important details, but the rest of your poem should contain description that helps readers feel what your experiences were like.

In the poem "A Blessing," American poet James Wright (1927–80) uses both details and description to place readers in a horse pasture and help them experience a moment of intense joy.

A Blessing

Just off the highway to Rochester, Minnesota,
Twilight bounds softly forth on the grass.
And the eyes of those two Indian ponies
Darken with kindness.
They have come gladly out of the willows
To welcome my friend and me.
We step over the barbed wire into the pasture
Where they have been grazing all day, alone.
They ripple tensely, they can hardly contain their happiness
That we have come.
They bow shyly as wet swans. They love each other.
There is no loneliness like theirs.
At home once more,
They begin munching the young tufts of spring in the darkness.
I would like to hold the slenderer one in my arms,
For she has walked over to me
And nuzzled my left hand.
She is black and white,
Her mane falls wild on her forehead,
And the light breeze moves me to caress her long ear
That is delicate as the skin over a girl's wrist.
Suddenly I realize
That if I stepped out of my body I would break
Into blossom.

In his poem, Wright provides some important details about the day. We know, for instance, that the poem takes place "off the highway to Rochester, Minnesota" and that the ponies were specifically Indian ponies. These details aren't anything that we can touch, but they help us understand the rest of Wright's descriptions even better. And this poem is rich with description. In fact, Wright involves readers in a complete scene, from the pasture at dusk to the actions of the ponies and the speaker.

Additionally, Wright uses striking imagery throughout his poem. He ends the poem with an image of his body bursting, like a flower, into blossom. What does this image make you think of, and how does it make you feel? Why do you think Wright ended his poem with this image?

You can create amazing poems if you remember the advice "Show, don't tell." Images have the power to involve your readers in your poems, no matter whether you use sensory description, similes, or metaphors. So keep your senses open and be ready to take in the world around you. Images abound. And when you read or write a well-constructed poem, they come alive!

Stanza Breaks

1. Activity: Personification. Place a common object from your house, such as a telephone or baseball glove, in front of you. Now, imagine the object coming to life. To personify it, give the object human actions and thoughts. Come up with at least 10 personifying images for the object, and try to combine these images into a poem.

2. Activity: Rewriting clichés. The following is a list of clichés. Try rewriting each overused phrase, making it into an original simile.

As hungry as a horse; Bright like the sun; As fast as lightning; As slow as a turtle; Dark like night; Quiet as a mouse; Red as a rose; and White as snow

3. Activity: Using your senses. Put pieces of fruit on a plate and use your senses to create interesting images. What does an apple smell like? What does it sound like when you bite into it? What does an orange look like? What does a pineapple feel like and taste like? Once you've written similes for your fruit, try rewriting them as metaphors. What's the effect?

4. Suggested Video: *Il Postino*. The Italian movie *Il Postino (The Postman)* tells the story of a poor Italian man who begins writing poetry when famous poet Pablo Neruda comes to town. The postman learns about using his senses to write similes and metaphors and feels a new world open up to him. Rated PG.

5. For More Information: William Carlos Williams. American poet William Carlos Williams was one of the leaders of the imagist movement, a movement that emphasized using images to express ideas. To find out more about Williams's life and read more of his poetry, see the Academy of American Poets Web site. The address is http://www.poets.org.

6. Activity: Metaphor fun with friends. Have each person write an emotion on one scrap of paper and an object on another, placing them in two separate hats. Taking turns, pick an emotion and an object and make an unexpected metaphor. For example, if you pick "happiness" and "car," your poem would start "Happiness is a car. . . ." To continue the thought, use description and imagery.

7. Activity: A poem about a person. Write about someone you care about, such as a family member or friend. Use description instead of details to make him or her come alive on the page. Think about how the person looks, smells, feels, and sounds. It's especially helpful to think of the person doing an activity so that you can show the person in action.

8. Activity: Walking with your eyes shut. After reading William Stafford's poem "Walking with Your Eyes Shut," write a poem using all of your senses *except* sight. You may try different locations, such as your backyard or the cafeteria at school. Unless you have someone leading you, *sitting* with your eyes shut may be safer!

9. Activity: Revision exercise. All poets revise, meaning they write and rewrite their poems to make them better. Look at the activities that you've done and pick out your favorite one. Revise this poem, paying close attention to your images. Are your images fresh? Do you use any clichés or mixed metaphors? Rewrite your poem until you think your images are the best they can be.

10. Activity: State of mind. Go to one of your favorite places. Now imagine getting straight As on your report card. Describe your favorite place with this mindset. After doing that, imagine your report card is filled with Ds and Fs. Again, describe your favorite place. Compare the two descriptions and see how your imagery changed, even though the actual place stayed the same.

Glossary

abstract: unclear, not specific, or unable to be defined by the senses; untouchable

clichés: images or phrases that have been overused and are no longer new

concrete: specific and able to be defined by sight, hearing, smell, taste, or touch

contemporary: of the present time

descriptions: information that involves the senses and clearly portrays an object

details: particular information that doesn't involve the senses and doesn't give readers a mental picture of the subject

metaphor: a type of image made by transferring the qualities of one object to another

mixed metaphors: conflicting images that don't work well together

personifying: giving an animal, plant, or object human characteristics and feelings

sensory: relating to one or more of the five senses

simile: a type of image made by comparing two subjects using like or as

sonnet: a 14-line poem that follows a special form

SELECTED WORKS

Bishop, Elizabeth. *The Complete Poems: 1927–1979.* New York: Farrar, Straus, and Giroux, 1984.

Dickinson, Emily. *The Collected Poems of Emily Dickinson*. New York: Random House, 1988.

Hughes, Langston. *The Collected Poems of Langston Hughes*. New York: Knopf, 1995.

Plath, Sylvia. *The Collected Poems*. New York: HarperCollins, 1981.

Rich, Adrienne. *Fact of a Doorframe: Poems 1956–2001*. New York: Norton, 2002.

Sandburg, Carl. *Selected Poems of Carl Sandburg*. New York: Random House, 1992.

Shakespeare, William. *The Sonnets*. New York: Penguin Classics, 2001.

Stafford, William. *The Way It Is: New and Selected Poems*. St. Paul, Minn.: Graywolf Press, 1999.

Williams, William Carlos. *Selected Poems*. New York: New Directions, 1985.

Wright, James. *Above the River: The Complete Poems*. Middletown, Conn.: Farrar, Straus, and Giroux, 1990.

INDEX

Date Due

BRODART Cat. No. 23 233 Printed in U.S.A.